BRITISH
WARSHIPS
AND AUXILIARIES

THE ROYAL NAVY

Some six years after the Berlin Wall came down, symbolically marking the end of the Cold War, the Royal Navy finds itself being worked harder than ever.

Since 1990 the fleet has suffered major cuts in frigate, submarine and mine countermeasures vessel numbers. Yet in the same period, a new "world disorder" has generated additional tasks and commitments, notably in the Adriatic arena.

Just prior to his leaving the navy in July 1995, Chief of Naval Staff and First Sea Lord Admiral Sir Benjamin Bathurst remarked that RN ships were in fact working harder on more overseas tasks than five years ago - with 30% fewer ships.

This mismatch in commitments and resources means ship programming is extremely taut, contingency is limited and overstretch is a constant concern. It is frequently considered a tribute to the RN's "can do" philosophy that it manages to get by. But the cost in terms of both men and material is mounting. There is a well rehearsed argument that it would do the RN no harm at all if it did in fact fail, publically, to meet a few commitments to let the Treasury (and taxpayers) realise the true state of affairs.Every other Government department seems to do so as a straight forward tactic to squeeze more cash from the Treasury.

Throughout 1995 the naval staff sought to bring some degree of stability back to naval life, only too aware of the turbulence of successive defence spending reviews. It is no secret that morale has been adversely affected by frequent and often radical change.

Breaches in sea/shore harmony objectives (which state that a ship should spend 40% of its time in its base port) have become an all too regular occurrence for many ships' companies. Coupled to an ongoing programme of redundancies, it is little wonder that morale is at its lowest ebb for years.

There are also concerns that manpower has been cut too thin, affecting "regeneration" in time of crisis.

Paradoxically, the service has by and large won the political battle as to its roles and missions in the post-Cold War era. The RN has successfully - and demonstrably - made the transition from a relatively narrow Cold War remit to a new focus on limited power projection.

One development above all - the acquisition of the Tomahawk land attack cruise missile - symbolises this new emphasis on extended reach. Tomahawk, will be fitted to selected Trafalgar (and later Batch 2 Trafalgar) submarines, giving the RN a capability to conduct precision strikes at targets several hundred miles inland - all delivered from a covert submarine. Approval for an initial purchase of 65 missiles was confirmed in September '95.

In justifying the shift in its roles and missions, the navy has articulated a compelling rationale for the role of maritime forces in an era of "violent peace". Virtues of endurance, sustainability, mobility, reach and autonomy have struck a chord. Above all else, defence planners today want options - and the navy gives them plenty.

The European dimension

The nature of the United Kingdom's role in Europe continues to split both public and politicians alike. One highly charged area is the emerging defence dimension for the European Community, thrust into the limelight after a controversial speech by Defence Secretary Michael Portillo at the 1995 Conservative Party conference.

Calls for closer European integration on maritime defence are already gaining ground through the Western European Union (WEU). At a WEU ministerial meeting in May '95, France, Italy and Spain signed the founding documents for the creation of a maritime joint task force to be known as EUROMARFOR (European Maritime force). Portugal immediately announced its decision to join EUROMARFOR, with membership also open to other full WEU members, although the RN currently has no plans to join on a permanent basis.

Of course, multinational standing naval forces are nothing new. NATO's Standing Naval Force Atlantic and Standing Naval Force Mediterranean have pioneered the concept, latterly proving their worth in embargo enforcement operations off former Yugoslavia.

But EUROMARFOR represents a first purely European naval force and, whilst it will be available for deployment under NATO, it remains outside the structure of the North Atlantic alliance. As such, it symbolises a small but significant step towards a more closely integrated European defence capability.

When asked about it's European credentials, the RN is quick to highlight the UK/Netherlands Landing Force, a fully integrated amphibious force. But senior officers, while frequently reiterating the RN's strong links with the US Navy, are keeping a watchful eye on developments in the WEU and the European Community. If a wider European naval force should ever come about, the RN must take a leading role, or else risk being left out in the cold.

Procurement policy under fire

GEC's takeover of VSEL has to a large extent undermined the Ministry of Defence's competitive procurement policy. Already owners of Yarrow Shipbuilders Ltd on the Clyde, GEC's acquisition of VSEL gives Lord Weinstock an effective stranglehold on competition. It seems that, increasingly, head-to-head competition will be replaced by a new single source No Acceptable Price-No Contract (NAPNOC) negotiations.

Moreover, GEC has achieved its market dominance at a time when the MoD is seeking to offload virtually all contract risk on to industry. It is thus hardly surprising that the MoD is finding its ceiling prices regularly exceeded when tenders are submitted.

If industry is expected to shoulder the full burden of (say) a nuclear submarine contract covering the build of up to five new boats, updates to existing boats and in-service support, then risk margins must be built in. The MoD would be foolish to think otherwise.

The main challenge to the dominance of GEC-Marine (the newly formed GEC subsidiary bringing together Yarrow, VSEL and NNC) will come from Vosper Thornycroft (VT) on the south coast. Long recognised for its skills as a builder of glass-reinforced plastic (GRP) minehunters, VT has more recently re-established its credibility as a builder of steel warships through export contracts with Oman and Qatar.

Against this background, the company has bid against Yarrow for the new batch of up to three Type 23 frigates."on offer". It is also seeking to open a second UK build stream for the Project Horizon collaborative frigate, and has designs on the Type 23 replacement/Future Escort programme in the longer term. In addition, VT is looking to team up with other shipyards for outsize contracts such as new hydrographic survey vessels and auxiliary oilers.

Of course, all this assumes that naval ship orders will remain in the UK. Those in the MoD who advocate the lease or purchase of US F-16 fighters for the RAF might just as easily consider foreign-built warships - built in foreign state-subsidised yards - to be an acceptable procurement option.

It was only a few years ago that the MoD was prepared to consider foreign-sourced GRP hulls for the Sandown class minehunters. Only vociferous lobbying from Vosper Thornycroft and Yarrow put paid to the idea. It is also worth remembering that the hull of HMS Ocean has been built by a Norwegian-owned yard.-albeit in Glasgow.

The UK may already be preparing to cede control of one strategic defence industry, namely sonar. Plans to merge the sonar interests of GEC-Marconi, Ferranti-Thomson Sonar Systems and France's Thomson Sintra have now reached an advanced stage.

The increasing emphasis on pan-European industrial joint ventures is not in question. At a time when markets are diminishing, it makes sense to consolidate and rationalise.

But the are grave concerns that French industry will take a majority stake in the new group, dominating its business strategy and depriving the UK of overall control of a most sensitive technology. Crucially, this could inflict long term damage on the close US/UK relationship in underwater warfare.

Decisions on the future commercial status of the Royal Dockyards are now imminent, with the two incumbent management teams - Babcock Rosyth Defence and Devonport Management Ltd (DML) - both seeking to purchase the respective dockyard sites. With current contracts to run the yards expiring in the spring an announcement is urgently needed .

Uncertainties remain however, not least the ultimate cost of modernising Devonport's facilities to cope with the proposed Trident submarine refits. The stricter demands of the Nuclear Installations Inspectorate mean that the price tag could now be over £500 million - more than that for the now-abandoned RD57 dock development at Rosyth.

Some major submarine refit work has already been transferred to Rosyth. Could the question of Devonport Trident refits yet reappear?

Future equipment

At the time of writing (Nov 1995), the RN was awaiting several key decisions on major equipment contracts. It is imperative that these come in the space of the next 12 months for two reasons: firstly, the fleet renewal programme is already behind schedule, with ageing submarines and assault ships being expected to soldier on into the next century; secondly, further delays may mean that major decisions are put off until after the,expected, 1997 general election. -and all that could entail.

The biggest procurement programme is the Batch 2 Trafalgar Class (B2TC) nuclear attack submarine, five of which are required to replace the fast tiring Swiftsure class from 2004 onwards. A prime contract award is due in July 1996, but to achieve that date the programme must first clear a number of obstacles.

First up is the Landing Platform Dock replacement (LPD(R)) programme, intended to provide two successors for the veteran assault ship FEARLESS and INTREPID. (Rumoured already to have the names of ALBION and BULWARK penciled in for them). The much delayed order is expected at the turn of the year, with VSEL and MoD hammering out a price after tough NAPNOC process.

4

The fact that the MoD had to resort to single source negotiations for LPD(R) puts another question mark over the validity of competition for large warships since the demise of Swan Hunter.

Yarrow and VT did also considered bidding. Unable to accommodate a ship of LPD(R) size in their existing pre-launch facilities, both companies explored the possibility of a joint bid with Belfast-based Harland & Wolff. However, neither yard was able to develop a suitable proposal as the basis of a response to the MoD.

It is understood that the NAPNOC negotiations with VSEL have shown up very different ideas of "acceptable price" to the extent that there may have been as much as £100 million per ship variance in the rival estimates -if MoD "informed rumours" are to be believed. Should a two-ship LPD(R) programme prove unaffordable, it is understood that the RN would order a single LPD(R) and then seek to buy a second Ocean class LPH.

Given the current paucity of amphibious shipping resources, reports that the MoD may seek to buy one or two roll-on/roll-off ferries are most welcome. With the British merchant fleet now so run down, the nucleus of an on-call sealift force for a joint rapid deployment force would be a most encouraging development. That is, provided that such assets are regarded as complements to - not replacements for - specialist amphibious shipping.

A consistently delayed order for up to three more Type 23 frigates was expected before the end of 1995. GEC's takeover of VSEL has seen the Barrow yard bow out of the competition in deference to Yarrow. The latter is now head-to-head with Vospers.

Although the RN had planned to cease production of the Type 23 at 16 ships, some fleet planners are arguing a case for ordering a further three ships. This would allow for the eventual replacement of the whole Type 22 Batch 2 ships, which are regarded as costly to man and operate. It would also help to maintain the UK's warship building industrial base, providing a bridge to the late-running Common Generation Frigate (CNGF) programme.

And what of CNGF? Delay after delay has finally resulted in an official acknowledgement that the planned December 2002 in-service date is simply unattainable. The fact that there is no official indication on the revised in service date is equally worrisome, although late 2004 seems a fair bet.

After much procrastination over the configuration, cost and workshare of the ship's Principal Anti-Air Missile System, it is hoped that the all-clear will be forthcoming for full-scale design definition work to begin in early 1996. The RN is seeking to buy 12 CNGFs - each displacing around 6,000 tonnes - to replace its Type 42 destroyer force on a one-for-one basis.

Beyond CNGF, work has already started on a post-2010 Type 22/23 frigate replacement - the so-called Future Escort. One radical innovation being examined in the context of this programme is the adoption of an unconventional trimaran hullform which proponents believe would offer better seakeeping, improved survivability and lower through-life costs.

On the mine countermeasures front, construction of HMS PENZANCE, the first of seven so-called Batch 2 Sandown class minehunters, began in September 1995 - all of 14 months after the contract award to Vosper Thornycroft was announced.

In fact, the last of these seven new vessels will not enter RN service until the year 2002. Only then will the UK's mine countermeasures fleet reach its stated 25-ship force level. The extended build schedule is not down to the shipbuilder, who would be happy to accelerate delivery if funding allowed, but the fault of a parsimonious MoD - held back by the Treasury of course.

The January 1995 award of a £40 million contract to BAeSEMA for the design and build of a new Ocean Survey Vessel (OSV) marked the first step to radically overhaul the RN's Hydrographic Surveying Squadron.

Back in 1993 the MoD undertook a detailed study of the specialist hydrographic capability required for RN operations in both peace and war. This took into account the changed requirements of the post-Cold War environment.

In May 1994 it was announced that the capability of the Squadron would be upgraded by the provision of four new commercially designed vessels - flying the white ensign - to replace existing hulls; these new ships, which will be larger than the existing vessels, will be either leased or owned by the MoD.

The first, a new Ocean Survey Vessel, to be named HMS SCOTT after the Antarctic explorer, is to be the largest of these four new vessels. Entering service in late 1997, the SCOTT will carry out hydrographic surveys throughout the world.

Orders for smaller hydrographic vessels should follow. However, there are already indications that only two of the planned three ships may now be funded.

Looking further ahead, pre-feasibility work continues to define the future structure of organic air beyond the first decade of the next century. Although new carrier technologies are being evaluated, the whole area is being considered as an overall package, driven in the main by the air power element.

Accordingly, the eventual replacement of the Sea Harrier is a key priority and there are important moves afoot to turn these aims into reality through participation in the US/UK collaborative Joint Strike Fighter programme. Also under consideration is a proposal to bring forward ARK ROYAL from lay up in Portsmouth dockyard - partially to provide an extra CVS to relieve the two currently operating back to back in the Adriatic - but probably more important is the requirement for the Treasury to see three vessels operating. When MoD is looking for long term finance to replace all three there is little likelihood of all the monies being forthcoming if the RN is managing to maintain its current commitments with just two ships. Should the proposal be taken up, finding the ships company - and air group - for a CVS after the current round of manpower economies will be another serious matter to address.

1996 promises to be a most interesting year - especially with a general election looming ever closer!

SHIPS OF THE ROYAL NAVY
Pennant Numbers

Ship	Pennant Number	Ship	Pennant Number
		LONDON	F95
Aircraft Carriers		SHEFFIELD	F96
		COVENTRY	F98
INVINCIBLE	R05	CORNWALL	F99
ILLUSTRIOUS	R06	LANCASTER	F229
ARK ROYAL ●	R07	NORFOLK	F230
		ARGYLL	F231
Destroyers		MARLBOROUGH	F233
		IRON DUKE	F234
BIRMINGHAM	D86	MONMOUTH	F235
NEWCASTLE	D87	MONTROSE	F236
GLASGOW	D88	WESTMINSTER	F237
EXETER	D89	NORTHUMBERLAND	F238
SOUTHAMPTON	D90	RICHMOND	F239
NOTTINGHAM	D91		
LIVERPOOL	D92	**Submarines**	
MANCHESTER	D95		
GLOUCESTER	D96	REPULSE	S23
EDINBURGH	D97	RENOWN	S26
YORK	D98	VANGUARD	S28
CARDIFF	D108	VICTORIOUS	S29
		VIGILANT	S30
Frigates		UPHOLDER ●	S40
		UNSEEN ●	S41
GRAFTON	F80	URSULA ●	S42
SUTHERLAND	F81	UNICORN ●	S43
SOMERSET	F82	TRENCHANT	S91
CUMBERLAND	F85	TALENT	S92
CAMPBELTOWN	F86	TRIUMPH	S93
CHATHAM	F87	SCEPTRE	S104
BATTLEAXE	F89	SPARTAN	S105
BRILLIANT	F90	SPLENDID	S106
BRAZEN	F91	TRAFALGAR	S107
BOXER	F92	SOVEREIGN	S108
BEAVER	F93	SUPERB	S109
BRAVE	F94		

Ship	Pennant Number	Ship	Pennant Number
TURBULENT	S110	STARLING	P241
TIRELESS	S117	LEEDS CASTLE	P258
TORBAY	S118	ARCHER	P264
		DUMBARTON CASTLE	P265
Assault Ships		BITER	P270
		SMITER	P272
FEARLESS	L10	PURSUER	P273
INTREPID ●	L11	ANGLESEY	P277
		ALDERNEY	P278
Minesweepers		BLAZER	P279
& Minehunters		DASHER	P280
		PUNCHER	P291
BRECON	M29	CHARGER	P292
LEDBURY	M30	RANGER	P293
CATTISTOCK	M31	TRUMPETER	P294
COTTESMORE	M32	GUERNSEY	P297
BROCKLESBY	M33	SHETLAND	P298
MIDDLETON	M34	ORKNEY	P299
DULVERTON	M35	LINDISFARNE	P300
BICESTER	M36		
CHIDDINGFOLD	M37	**Survey Ships & RN**	
ATHERSTONE	M38	**Manned Auxiliaries**	
HURWORTH	M39		
BERKELEY	M40	BRITANNIA	A00
QUORN	M41	GLEANER	A86
SANDOWN	M101	ROEBUCK	A130
INVERNESS	M102	HECLA	A133
CROMER	M103	HERALD	A138
WALNEY	M104	LOYAL WATCHER	A159
BRIDPORT	M105	EXPRESS	A163
BLACKWATER	M2008	EXPLORER	A164
ITCHEN	M2009	EXAMPLE	A165
ORWELL	M2011	EXPLOIT	A167
SPEY	M2013	ENDURANCE	A171
ARUN	M2014	IRONBRIDGE	A311
		BULLDOG	A317
Patrol Craft		IXWORTH	A318
PEACOCK	P239	BEAGLE	A319
PLOVER	P240	LOYAL CHANCELLOR	A1770
		● *Ships in reserve/long refit*	

KEEP UP TO DATE
THROUGHOUT THE YEAR

Warship World is published each quarter and gives you all the information necessary to keep this book updated throughout the year. See inside front cover for details.

HMS Vanguard

VANGUARD CLASS

Ship	Pennant Number	Completion Date	Builder
VANGUARD	S28	1992	VSEL
VICTORIOUS	S29	1994	VSEL
VIGILANT	S30	1996	VSEL
VENGEANCE	S31	1998	VSEL

Displacement 15,000 tons (dived) **Dimensions** 150m x 13m x 12m **Speed** 25 + dived **Armament** 16 - Trident 2 (D5) missiles, 4 Torpedo Tubes **Complement** 135 (2 crews).

Notes
VANGUARD and VICTORIOUS were both operational by end of 1995.

● OFFICIAL PHOTO

HMS Renown

RESOLUTION CLASS

Ship	Pennant Number	Completion Date	Builder
REPULSE	S23	1968	Vickers
RENOWN	S26	1968	C. Laird

Displacement 8,400 tons (submerged) **Dimensions** 130m x 10m x 9m **Speed** 25 knots **Armament** 16 Polaris missiles, 6 Torpedo Tubes **Complement** 147 (Two crews).

Notes

These last two nuclear-powered Polaris submarines have been the United Kingdom's contribution to NATO's strategic nuclear deterrent since the late 1960's. Despite their age one of these submarines has been kept constantly on patrol. Thanks to their high speed, long endurance underwater, and advanced sonar and electronic equipment they have had little fear of detection.

RENOWN will decommission in early 1996. REPULSE will continue in service until the late 1990's.

● HMS NEPTUNE

HMS Sceptre

SWIFTSURE CLASS

Ship	Pennant Number	Completion Date	Builder
SCEPTRE	S104	1978	Vickers
SPARTAN	S105	1979	Vickers
SPLENDID	S106	1980	Vickers
SOVEREIGN	S108	1974	Vickers
SUPERB	S109	1976	Vickers

Displacement 4,500 tons dived **Dimensions** 83m x 10m x 8m **Speed** 30 knots + dived **Armament** 5 Torpedo Tubes **Complement** 116.

Notes
All are based at Faslane. SWIFTSURE is awaiting disposal at Rosyth. SPARTAN was to have been placed in reserve for 3 years but these plans have now been abandoned. The class will be replaced in due course by the Batch 2 Trafalgar boats.

HMS Triumph

TRAFALGAR CLASS

Ship	Pennant Number	Completion Date	Builder
TRENCHANT	S91	1989	Vickers
TALENT	S92	1990	Vickers
TRIUMPH	S93	1991	Vickers
TRAFALGAR	S107	1983	Vickers
TURBULENT	S110	1984	Vickers
TIRELESS	S117	1985	Vickers
TORBAY	S118	1986	Vickers

Displacement 4,500 tons **Dimensions** 85m x 10m x 8m **Speed** 30 + dived **Armament** 5 Torpedo Tubes **Complement** 125.

Notes
Enhanced development of the Swiftsure Class. Quieter, faster and with greater endurance than their predecessors. Tomahawk Cruise Missiles will eventually be fitted in these boats. Three new, Batch 2, Trafalgar Class are expected to be ordered in early 1996 and a further two at a later date.

UPHOLDER CLASS

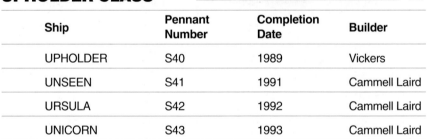

Ship	Pennant Number	Completion Date	Builder
UPHOLDER	S40	1989	Vickers
UNSEEN	S41	1991	Cammell Laird
URSULA	S42	1992	Cammell Laird
UNICORN	S43	1993	Cammell Laird

Displacement 2,400 tons (dived) **Dimensions** 70m x 8m x 5m **Speed** 20 knots dived **Armament** 6 Torpedo Tubes: Sub Harpoon missile **Complement** 44.

Notes

A new class of conventionally powered submarines. As a result of Defence economies announced in 1993 all the class have been actively marketed for sale/lease overseas.They were paid off during 1994 and are laid up at Barrow-in-Furness.

14

● OFFICIAL PHOTO

HMS Illustrious

INVINCIBLE CLASS

Ship	Pennant Number	Completion Date	Builder
INVINCIBLE	R05	1979	Vickers
ILLUSTRIOUS	R06	1982	Swan Hunter
ARK ROYAL	R07	1985	Swan Hunter

Displacement 19,500 tons **Dimensions** 206m x 32m x 6.5m **Speed** 28 knots **Armament** Sea Dart Missile, 2 - 20mm guns, 3 Phalanx/Goalkeeper **Aircraft** 8 - Sea Harrier, 12 - Sea King **Complement** 900 + aircrews.

Notes
Manpower problems have dictated that only two ships are kept in the operational fleet, with the third in refit or reserve. Both have operated 'back to back' in the Adriatic throughout 1995. ARK ROYAL in reserve at Portsmouth but may be brought forward for further service before scheduled refit

15

The shape of things to come.....
The future HMS OCEAN

● OFFICIAL PHOTO

HMS Ocean

Displacement 20,000 tons **L.O.A.** 203m **Speed** 19 knots **Complement** Ship 258, Squadrons 180, Embarked force 800.

Notes
Launched in October 1995 at Kvaerner's yard in Glasgow. Will be fitted out by VSEL at Barrow in 1997.

● OFFICIAL PHOTO

HMS Fearless

FEARLESS CLASS

Ship	Pennant Number	Completion Date	Builder
FEARLESS	L10	1965	Harland & Wolff
INTREPID	L11	1967	J. Brown

Displacement 12,500 tons, 19,500 tons (flooded) **Dimensions** 158m x 24m x 8m **Speed** 20 knots **Armament** 2 Sea Cat Missile Systems, 2 - 40mm guns, 4 - 30mm + 2 - 20mm (INTREPID only) 2 - Vulcan Phalanx (FEARLESS only) **Complement** 580.

Notes
Multi-purpose ships that can operate helicopters for embarked Royal Marine Commandos. 4 landing craft are carried on an internal deck and are flooded out when the ship docks down. INTREPID paid off in 1991 when a decision was made that both vessels would be replaced. Financial restraints have delayed any order being made but it was expected at the end of 1995. As a result of their age both ships have become extremely expensive to keep operational. Limited refitting work has been undertaken onboard INTREPID and it was thought most unlikely she would ever operate at sea again. However, the situation in Bosnia and the requirement to withdraw from Hong Kong in 1997 may alter this.

17

● OFFICIAL PHOTO

HMS Birmingham

SHEFFIELD CLASS
(Type 42) Batch 1 & 2

Ship	Pennant Number	Completion Date	Builder
BIRMINGHAM	D86	1976	C. Laird
NEWCASTLE	D87	1978	Swan Hunter
GLASGOW	D88	1978	Swan Hunter
EXETER	D89	1980	Swan Hunter
SOUTHAMPTON	D90	1981	Vosper T.
NOTTINGHAM	D91	1982	Vosper T.
LIVERPOOL	D92	1982	C. Laird
CARDIFF	D108	1979	Vickers

Displacement 3,660 tons **Dimensions** 125m x 15m x 7m **Speed** 29 knots **Armament** 1 - 4.5" gun, 4 - 20mm guns, Sea Dart Missile System: 2 - Phalanx, Lynx Helicopter, 6 Torpedo Tubes **Complement** 280 +.

Notes
Sister Ships SHEFFIELD and COVENTRY lost in 1982 during the Falklands conflict. All have seen extensive service in the Gulf and Adriatic throughout 1995.

HMS Gloucester

SHEFFIELD CLASS
(Type 42) Batch 3

Ship	Pennant Number	Completion Date	Builder
MANCHESTER	D95	1983	Vickers
GLOUCESTER	D96	1984	Vosper T.
EDINBURGH	D97	1985	C. Laird
YORK	D98	1984	Swan Hunter

Displacement 4,775 tons **Dimensions** 132m x 15m x 7m **Speed** 30 knots + **Armament** 1- 4.5" gun, 1- Phalanx, 4 - 20mm guns. Sea Dart missile system. Lynx Helicopter, 6 Torpedo Tubes **Complement** 301.

Notes
"Stretched' versions of earlier ships of this class. Designed to provide area defence of a task force. Deck edge stiffening fitted to counter increased hull stress. Studies continue(with France & Italy) on the requirement for a Common New Generation Frigate to enter service in 2004.

● OFFICIAL PHOTO

HMS Battleaxe

BROADSWORD CLASS
(Type 22) Batch 1

Ship	Pennant Number	Completion Date	Builder
BATTLEAXE	F89	1980	Yarrow
BRILLIANT	F90	1981	Yarrow
BRAZEN	F91	1982	Yarrow

Displacement 3,860 tons **Dimensions** 131m x 15m x 6m **Speed** 29 knots **Armament** 4 Exocet Missiles, 2 Sea Wolf Missile Systems, 4 - 30mm guns, 2 or 4 - 20mm guns, 6 Torpedo Tubes, 2 Lynx Helicopters **Complement** 224.

Notes
Although capable of carrying 2 helicopters, only 1 normally embarked. BROADSWORD sold to Brazil in 1995. Remainder of class have also been sold to Brazil, in a £100 million deal, for delivery in 1996/97.

● OFFICIAL PHOTO

HMS Coventry

BROADSWORD CLASS
(Type 22) Batch 2

Ship	Pennant Number	Completion Date	Builder
BOXER	F92	1983	Yarrow
BEAVER	F93	1984	Yarrow
BRAVE•	F94	1985	Yarrow
LONDON •	F95	1986	Yarrow
SHEFFIELD •	F96	1987	Swan Hunter
COVENTRY •	F98	1988	Swan Hunter

Displacement 4,100 tons **Dimensions** 143m x 15m x 6m **Speed** 30 knots **Armament** 4 Exocet Missiles, 2 Sea Wolf Missile Systems, 4 - 30mm + 2 - 20mm guns, 6 Torpedo Tubes, 2 Lynx Helicopters **Complement** 273.

Notes
• Ships have enlarged hangar and flight deck. A Sea King can be, and is, carried in some ships of this class.All ships have an intelligence gathering capability.

21

HMS Chatham

BROADSWORD CLASS
(Type 22) Batch 3

Ship	Pennant Number	Completion Date	Builder
CUMBERLAND	F85	1988	Yarrow
CAMPBELTOWN	F86	1988	C. Laird
CHATHAM	F87	1989	Swan Hunter
CORNWALL	F99	1987	Yarrow

Displacement 4,200 tons **Dimensions** 147m x 15m x 7m **Speed** 30 knots **Armament** 1 - 4.5" gun, 1 - Goalkeeper, 8- Harpoon, 2- Seawolf, 4 - 30mm guns, 6 Torpedo Tubes, 2 Lynx or 1 Sea King Helicopter **Complement** 250.

Notes
General purpose gun and Goalkeeper system added to these ships as a direct result of lessons learned during Falklands conflict. All these ships have a major anti-submarine capability. Cost £180 million each.

22

• ROYAL AUSTRALIAN NAVY

HMS Monmouth

23

Photo see page 23

DUKE CLASS (Type 23)

Ship	Pennant Number	Completion Date	Builder
GRAFTON	F80	1996	Yarrow
SUTHERLAND	F81	1997	Yarrow
SOMERSET	F82	1996	Yarrow
LANCASTER	F229	1991	Yarrow
NORFOLK	F230	1989	Yarrow
ARGYLL	F231	1991	Yarrow
MARLBOROUGH	F233	1991	Swan Hunter
IRON DUKE	F234	1992	Yarrow
MONMOUTH	F235	1993	Yarrow
MONTROSE	F236	1993	Yarrow
WESTMINSTER	F237	1993	Swan Hunter
NORTHUMBERLAND	F238	1994	Swan Hunter
RICHMOND	F239	1994	Swan Hunter

Displacement 3,500 tons **Dimensions** 133m x 15m x 5m **Speed** 28 knots **Armament** Harpoon & Seawolf missile systems: 1 - 4.5" gun, 4 - 2 twin, magazine launched, Torpedo Tubes **Complement** 157.

Notes
An invitation to tender was placed in late 1995 for three more vessels. 23 ships had been planned for the class but no further orders will be placed after this last batch have been delivered.

HMS Atherstone

MINE COUNTERMEASURES SHIPS (MCMV'S) HUNT CLASS

Ship	Pennant Number	Completion Date	Builder
BRECON	M29	1980	Vosper T.
LEDBURY	M30	1981	Vosper T.
CATTISTOCK	M31	1982	Vosper T.
COTTESMORE	M32	1983	Yarrow
BROCKLESBY	M33	1983	Vosper T.
MIDDLETON	M34	1984	Yarrow
DULVERTON	M35	1983	Vosper T.
BICESTER	M36	1986	Vosper T.
CHIDDINGFOLD	M37	1984	Vosper T.
ATHERSTONE	M38	1987	Vosper T.
HURWORTH	M39	1985	Vosper T.
BERKELEY	M40	1988	Vosper T.
QUORN	M41	1989	Vosper T.

Displacement 625 tonnes **Dimensions** 60m x 10m x 2.2m **Speed** 17 knots **Armament** 1 x 30mm + 2 x 20mm guns **Complement** 45.

Notes

The largest warships ever built of glass reinforced plastic. Their cost (£35m each) has dictated the size of the class. Very sophisticated ships – and lively seaboats! Some vessels are used in a Fishery Protection role. All based at Portsmouth and Faslane.

HMS Arun

FLEET MINESWEEPERS
RIVER CLASS

Ship	Pennant Number	Completion Date	Builder
BLACKWATER	M2008	1985	Richards
ITCHEN	M2009	1985	Richards
ORWELL	M2011	1985	Richards
SPEY	M2013	1985	Richards
ARUN	M2014	1986	Richards

Displacement 850 tonnes **Dimensions** 47m x 10m x 3m **Speed** 14 knots **Armament** 1 - 40mm + 2 - GPMG **Complement** 30.

Notes

MCM ships built for service with the RNR. All were withdrawn during 1994 as a result of the 1993 defence economies. All are employed in the Northern Ireland Squadron (without pennant numbers) except ORWELL which is a training ship attached to BRNC Dartmouth.

● DANE MURDOCH

HMS Sandown

SANDOWN CLASS

Ship	Pennant Number	Completion Date	Builder
SANDOWN	M101	1989	Vosper T.
INVERNESS	M102	1991	Vosper T.
CROMER	M103	1991	Vosper T.
WALNEY	M104	1992	Vosper T.
BRIDPORT	M105	1993	Vosper T.

Displacement 450 tons **Dimensions** 53m x 10m x 2m **Speed** 13 knots **Armament** 1 - 30mm gun **Complement** 34.

Notes
A class dedicated to a single mine hunting role. Propulsion is by vectored thrust and bow thrusters. Up to 15 more ships were planned, but the 7 due to be ordered in 1991 were postponed until 1994. They will be named (acceptance dates in brackets) PEN-ZANCE (97), PEMBROKE (98), GRIMSBY (99), BANGOR (00), RAMSEY (00), BLYTH (01), SHOREHAM (01)

● D HANNAFORD

HMS Dumbarton Castle

CASTLE CLASS

Ship	Pennant Number	Completion Date	Builder
LEEDS CASTLE	P258	1981	Hall Russell
DUMBARTON CASTLE	P265	1982	Hall Russell

Displacement 1,450 tons **Dimensions** 81m x 11m x 3m **Speed** 20 knots **Armament** 1 - 40mm gun **Complement** 40.

Notes

These ships have a dual role – that of fishery protection and offshore patrols within the limits of UK territorial waters. Unlike the Island Class these ships are able to operate helicopters – including Sea King aircraft. Trials have been conducted to assess the suitability of these ships as Minelayers. LEEDS CASTLE is on long term deployment to the Falkland Islands with her ships' company rotating every four months.

HMS Guernsey

ISLAND CLASS

Ship	Pennant Number	Completion Date	Builder
ANGLESEY	P277	1979	Hall Russell
ALDERNEY	P278	1979	Hall Russell
GUERNSEY	P297	1977	Hall Russell
SHETLAND	P298	1977	Hall Russell
ORKNEY	P299	1977	Hall Russell
LINDISFARNE	P300	1978	Hall Russell

Displacement 1,250 tons **Dimensions** 60m x 11m x 4m **Speed** 17 knots **Armament** 1 - 40mm gun **Complement** 39.

Notes

Built on trawler lines these ships were introduced to protect the extensive British interests in North Sea oil/gas installations and to patrol the 200 mile fishery limit. All vessels have extra crew members to allow leave to be taken and thus extend vessels time on task over the year.

● OFFICIAL PHOTO

HMS Peacock

PEACOCK CLASS

Ship	Pennant Number	Completion Date	Builder
PEACOCK	P239	1983	Hall Russell
PLOVER	P240	1983	Hall Russell
STARLING	P241	1984	Hall Russell

Displacement 700 tons **Dimensions** 60m x 10m x 5m **Speed** 28 knots **Armament** 1 - 76mm gun **Complement** 31.

Notes

The first warships to carry the 76mm Oto Melara gun. They are used to provide an ocean going back-up to the Marine Department of the Hong Kong Police. The Government of Hong Kong paid 75% of the building and maintenance costs of these vessels. Sister ships SWALLOW and SWIFT returned to UK in 1988 and were sold (Oct 88) to the Irish Navy after only 3 years RN service. All three vessels are expected to remain in Hong Kong until the withdrawal in 1997 and may then be sold.

HMS Puncher

COASTAL TRAINING CRAFT
ARCHER CLASS

Ship	Pennant Number	Completion Date	Builder
ARCHER	P264	1985	Watercraft
BITER	P270	1985	Watercraft
SMITER	P272	1986	Watercraft
PURSUER	P273	1988	Vosper
BLAZER	P279	1988	Vosper
DASHER	P280	1988	Vosper
PUNCHER	P291	1988	Vosper
CHARGER	P292	1988	Vosper
RANGER	P293	1988	Vosper
TRUMPETER	P294	1988	Vosper

Displacement 43 tonnes **Dimensions** 20m x 6m x 1m **Speed** 20 knots **Armament** Nil **Complement** 14.

Notes
In service with RN University units. TRUMPETER and RANGER deployed to Gibraltar in 1991.

● D HANNAFORD

HMS Roebuck

ROEBUCK CLASS

Ship	Pennant Number	Completion Date	Builder
ROEBUCK	A130	1986	Brooke Marine

Displacement 1500 tonnes **Dimensions** 64m x 13m x 4m **Speed** 15 knots **Complement** 47.

Notes
Was due to replace HECLA in the Survey fleet until the latter reprieved in 1987 for further service. Fitted with the latest fixing aids and sector scanning sonar. An order for new vessels to replace ROEBUCK and BEAGLE/BULLDOG is expected during 1996.

HMS Herald

HECLA CLASS

Ship	Pennant Number	Completion Date	Builder
HECLA	A133	1965	Yarrow
HERALD	A138	1974	Robb Caledon

Displacement 2,733 tons **Dimensions** 79m x 15m x 5m **Speed** 14 knots **Complement** 115.

Notes

Able to operate for long periods away from shore support, these ships and the smaller ships of the Hydrographic Fleet collect the data that is required to produce the Admiralty Charts and publications which are sold to mariners worldwide. A new (13,500 ton) vessel to replace HECLA was ordered from Appledore Shipbuilders in 1995. Due for completion in 1997 she will be named SCOTT (A131).

HMS Bulldog

BULLDOG CLASS

Ship	Pennant Number	Completion Date	Builder
BULLDOG	A317	1968	Brooke Marine
BEAGLE	A319	1968	Brooke Marine

Displacement 1,088 tons **Dimensions** 60m x 11m x 4m **Speed** 15 knots **Complement** 39.

Notes
Designed to operate in coastal waters. Both have been extensively refitted to extend hull life. GLEANER (A86) is a small inshore survey craft based at Portsmouth.

HMY Britannia

ROYAL YACHT

Ship	Pennant Number	Completion Date	Builder
BRITANNIA	A00	1954	J. Brown

Displacement 5,280 tons **Dimensions** 126m x 17m x 5m **Speed** 21 knots **Complement** 250.

Notes
Probably the best known ship in the Royal Navy, BRITANNIA was designed to be converted to a hospital ship in time of war but this conversion was not made during the Falklands or Gulf crisis and the role has now been abandoned. Due to be paid off in 1997.

● OFFICIAL PHOTO

HMS Endurance

ICE PATROL SHIP

Ship	Pennant Number	Completion Date	Builder
ENDURANCE	A171	1990	Ulstein-Hatlo

Displacement 5,129 tons **Dimensions** 91m x 17.9m x 6.5m **Speed** 14.9 knots **Armament** Small arms **Aircraft** 2 Lynx **Complement** 113.

Notes
Chartered for only 7 months in late 1991 to replace the older vessel of the same name. Originally M/V POLAR CIRCLE, renamed HMS POLAR CIRCLE (A176) and then purchased by MOD(N) and renamed again in October 1992 to current name.

● W SARTORI

Loyal Chancellor

LOYAL CLASS

Ship	Pennant Number	Ship	Pennant Number
LOYAL WATCHER	A159	LOYAL CHANCELLOR	A1770

G.R.T. 112 tons **Dimensions** 24m x 6m x 3m **Speed** 10.5 knots **Complement** 24.

Notes
Former RNXS craft now used by the RN university units at Oxford and Cambridge.

● OFFICIAL PHOTO

Example

COASTAL TRAINING CRAFT
EXAMPLE CLASS

Ship	Pennant Number	Completion Date	Builder
EXPRESS	A163	1988	Vosper T
EXPLORER	A164	1985	Watercraft
EXAMPLE	A165	1985	Watercraft
EXPLOIT	A167	1988	Vosper T

Displacement 43 tons **Dimensions** 20m x 6m x 1m **Speed** 20 knots **Armament** Nil
Complement 14

Notes
Training vessels for the RNXS - until the organisation was disbanded on 31March 1994. Vessels were then transferred to RN University Units as sea training tenders.

Northella

Ship	Pennant Number	Completion Date	Builder
NORTHELLA		1973	Clelands

G.R.T. 1,535 **Dimensions** 77m x 12.7m x 6m **Speed** 15 knots **Complement** 14

Notes
Former deep water stern trawler owned by Marr's of Hull. Taken up from trade for the Falklands Conflict in 1982 (as a minesweeper) and again in 1983 as a target vessel. In 1985 again chartered for service as a Navigational Training Vessel. Charters have been renewed since then and vessel has been successfully used in a number of secondary roles. Can carry up to 20 trainees.

Colonel Templer

Ship	Pennant Number	Completion Date	Builder
COLONEL TEMPLER		1966	Hall Russell

Displacement 1,300 tons **Dimensions** 56m x 11m x 5.6 m **Speed** 12 knots
Complement 14

Notes

Built as a stern trawler but converted in 1980 for use by the Defence Research Agency as an acoustic research vessel. A major rebuild was completed after a serious fire gutted the vessel in 1990. Up to 12 scientists can be carried.

A number of merchant ships are on charter to various MOD departments. They include MAERSK GANNET, MAERSK ASCENCION, ST BRANDAN, INDOMITABLE and OIL MARINER in support of the Falkland Island commitment. PROUD SEAHORSE and MARINE EXPLORER have hydrographic, training/trials roles in UK waters.

THE ROYAL FLEET AUXILIARY

The Royal Fleet Auxiliary Service (RFA) is a civilian manned fleet owned and operated by the Ministry of Defence. Its main task is to supply warships of the Royal Navy at sea with fuel, food, stores and ammunition which they need to remain operational while away from base.The service also provides aviation support and training facilities for the Royal Navy – together with amphibious support and secure sea transport for army units. NATO warships are frequent "customers" too (on a repayment basis).

The service prides itself that each ship is available for operations for approximately 80% of the year. Unlike the RN, officers and men of the RFA join a vessel for a period of time - say six months - and do not expect to be in port for leave periods at all during this period. In due course they are themselves relieved on board before heading home for a (lengthy) period of leave and eventually another ship. This practice of course ensures that the RFA's ships can be used to the maximum and are not seen spending weeks alongside in a base with their crew on leave.- as frequently happens to an RN ship. (This practice would hardly work on a "High Tech" RN ship where pre-joining training, work up etc would make such a rapid turn round of trained personnel at sea simply inefficient)

Throughout 1995 the service had a standing commitment to provide tankers, carrying the ever vital fuel, in the West Indies, Falklands, Gulf and Adriatic. As can be seen from the following pages to provide this level of service with the number of operational hulls available - and fulfil training and exercise requirements too - is not easy. "Tanker stretch" is a pressing issue and the price is now being paid for past policies which have simply been "Big is beautiful". We now see massive RFA's having to be deployed to support single RN ship operations - whilst the ever useful (but small) Rover Class continue to be sold off. No doubt "Treasurythink" says let them have one big vessel rather than two small ones - as it makes economic sense (one crew, one fuel bill etc etc). "Operational flexibility" doesn't mean too much to the pen pushers...

Having survived the "Front Line First" study now is the time to radically appraise the real long term requirements of the customer - a much smaller, but widely deployed, Royal Navy.

SHIPS OF THE ROYAL FLEET AUXILIARY
Pennant Numbers

Ship	Pennant Number	Ship	Pennant Number	Ship	Pennant Number
BRAMBLELEAF	A81	ARGUS	A135	FORT GEORGE	A388
BAYLEAF	A109	GREY ROVER	A269	RESOURCE	A480
ORANGELEAF	A110	GOLD ROVER	A271	SIR BEDIVERE	L3004
OAKLEAF	A111	BLACK ROVER	A273	SIR GALAHAD	L3005
OLWEN	A122	FORT GRANGE	A385	SIR GERAINT	L3027
OLNA	A123	FORT AUSTIN	A386	SIR PERCIVALE	L3036
DILIGENCE	A132	FORT VICTORIA	A387	SIR TRISTRAM	L3505

●D HANNAFORD

RFA Olna

'OL' CLASS

Ship	Pennant Number	Completion Date	Builder
OLWEN	A122	1965	Hawthorn Leslie
OLNA	A123	1966	Hawthorn Leslie

Displacement 36,000 tons **Dimensions** 197m x 26m x 10m **Speed** 19 knots **Complement** 92.

Notes

These ships can operate up to 3 Sea King helicopters.-and are frequently used for Helicopter training when ARGUS is not available. Dry stores can be carried – and transferred at sea – as well as a wide range of fuel, aviation spirit and lubricants. Both due to be replaced in 2000/01.

● D HANNAFORD

RFA Black Rover

ROVER CLASS

Ship	Pennant Number	Completion Date	Builder
GREY ROVER ●	A269	1970	Swan Hunter
GOLD ROVER	A271	1974	Swan Hunter
BLACK ROVER	A273	1974	Swan Hunter

Displacement 11,522 tons **Dimensions** 141m x 19m x 7m **Speed** 18 knots
Armament 2 - 20mm guns **Complement** 49/54

Notes
Small Fleet Tankers designed to supply HM ships with fresh water, dry cargo and refrigerated provisions as well as a range of fuel and lubricants. Helicopter deck but no hangar. ● For disposal 1997.

RFA Orangeleaf

LEAF CLASS

Ship	Pennant Number	Completion Date	Builder
BRAMBLELEAF	A81	1980	Cammell Laird
BAYLEAF	A109	1982	Cammell Laird
ORANGELEAF	A110	1982	Cammell Laird
OAKLEAF	A111	1981	Uddevalla V

Displacement 37,747 tons **Dimensions** 170m x 26m x 12m **Speed** 14.5 knots **Complement** 60.

Notes
All are ex merchant ships & are.mainly employed on freighting duties BRAMBLELEAF is owned by MOD (N), the remainder are on charter. OAKLEAF differs from the other ships of the class which are all commercial Stat 32 tankers. At 49,310 tons she is the largest vessel in RFA/RN service. APPLELEAF taken over by the Royal Australian Navy (as HMAS Westralia) in late 1989.

44

● OFFICIAL PHOTO

RFA Fort Grange

FORT CLASS I

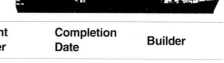

Ship	Pennant Number	Completion Date	Builder
FORT GRANGE	A385	1978	Scott Lithgow
FORT AUSTIN	A386	1979	Scott Lithgow

Displacement 23,384 tons **Dimensions** 183m x 24m x 9m **Speed** 20 knots **Complement** 201, (120 RFA, 36 RNSTS & 45 RN).

Notes
Full hangar and maintenance facilities are provided and up to four Sea King helicopters can be carried for both the transfer of stores and anti-submarine protection of a group of ships. Both ships can be armed with 4 - 20mm guns mounted on the Scot platforms. Both are fitted with 3" Chaff Systems.

● W SARTORI

RFA Fort George

FORT CLASS II

Ship	Pennant Number	Completion Date	Builder
FORT VICTORIA	A387	1992	Harland & Wolff
FORT GEORGE	A388	1993	Swan Hunter

Displacement 31,500 tons **Dimensions** 204m x 30m x 9m **Speed** 20 knots **Armament** 4 - 30mm guns, Sea Wolf Missile System (Fitted for but not with) **Complement** 100 (RFA), 24 civilians, 32 RN and up to 122 aircrew.

Notes

"One stop" replenishment ships with the widest range of armaments, fuel and spares carried. Can operate up to 5 Sea King Helicopters with full maintenance facilities onboard. Delays at the builder resulted in the plans for FORT VICTORIA to enter service in 1992 being abandoned. Both vessels eventually entered service after a series of delays in 1994.

RFA Resource

REGENT CLASS

Ship	Pennant Number	Completion Date	Builder
RESOURCE	A480	1967	Scotts

Displacement 23,256 tons **Dimensions** 195m x 24m x 8m **Speed** 21 knots **Armament** 2 - 20mm guns **Complement** 160, (RFA 112, RNSTS 37, RN 11).

Notes
The widest range of naval armament stores are carried onboard plus a limited range of general naval stores and food. When the Wessex 5 was withdrawn from service in April 1987 the ship lost its permanently embarked helicopter but retains full flight deck facilities. RESOURCE reverted to Reserve (Preservation by Operation) status at Rosyth in November 1991 but brought forward in late 1992 for service in the Adriatic.She remained at Split throughout 1993/5 returning to UK for a brief refit in 1994. Expected to return to UK and "extended readiness" during 1996.

RFA Sir Percivale

LANDING SHIPS (LOGISTIC) SIR LANCELOT CLASS

Ship	Pennant Number	Completion Date	Builder
SIR BEDIVERE	L3004	1967	Hawthorn
SIR GALAHAD	L3005	1987	Swan Hunter
SIR GERAINT	L3027	1967	Stephen
SIR PERCIVALE	L3036	1968	Hawthorn
SIR TRISTRAM	L3505	1967	Hawthorn

Displacement 5,550 tons **Dimensions** 126m x 18m x 4m **Speed** 17 knots **Armament** Can be fitted with 20 or 40mm guns in emergency **Complement** 65, (SIR GALAHAD is larger at 8,451 tons. 140m x 20m **Complement** 58).

Notes
Manned by the RFA but tasked by the Army, these ships are used for heavy secure transport of stores – embarked by bow and stern doors – and beach assault landings. Can operate helicopters from both vehicle and flight deck if required-and carry 340 troops. SIR TRISTRAM was rebuilt after extensive Falklands War damage. SIR BEDIVERE is expected to complete a Ship Life Extension Programme (SLEP) at Rosyth in 1996 which will see the vessel lengthened and considerably updated. Others are expected to follow, although the purchase of HMAS TOBRUK is being considered as an alternative

HMS Birmingham

HM Ships Ark Royal (L) and Illustrious

HM Ships Manchester (R) and Montrose (L)

A Squadron of
Sea Harriers (F/A2)

HMS Lindisfarne off Gibraltar

HMS Hurworth

RFA Olwen

RFA Fort Victoria

FORT VICTORIA
LONDON
A387

RFA Diligence

Ship	Pennant Number	Completion Date	Builder
DILIGENCE	A132	1981	Oesundsvarvet

Displacement 5,814 tons **Dimensions** 120m x 12m x 3m **Speed** 15 knots **Armament** 2 - 20mm **Complement** RFA 40, RN Personnel – approx 100.

Notes

Formerly the M/V STENA INSPECTOR purchased (£25m) for service in the South Atlantic. Her deep diving complex was removed and workshops added. Has given valuable support to a wide range of warships in the Falklands and Gulf. Acted as depot ship for a lengthy SSN deployment to the Far East during 1995.

RFA Argus

Ship	Pennant Number	Completion Date	Builder
ARGUS	A135	1981	Cantieri Navali Breda

Displacement 28,081 tons (full load) **Dimensions** 175m x 30m x 8m **Speed** 18 knots **Armament** 4 - 30 mm, 2 - 20 mm **Complement** 254 (inc 137 Air Group) **Aircraft** 6 Sea King, 12 Harriers can be carried in a "ferry role".

Notes

Formerly the M/V CONTENDER BEZANT taken up from trade during the Falklands crisis. Purchased in 1984 (£13 million) for conversion to an 'Aviation Training Ship'. A £50 million re-build was undertaken at Belfast from 1984-87. Undertook rapid conversion in October 1990 to "Primary Casualty Reception Ship" (Hospital Ship!) for service in the Gulf. These facilities remain "mothballed" on board for activation if required.

ROYAL MARITIME AUXILIARY SERVICE

The R M A S Fleet is administered by the Director of Marine Services (Naval) who is responsible for the provision of a wide range of Marine Services to the RN/RFA Fleet - and other users in the MoD and other Government departments.

Ships of the RMAS, which can be seen at work in the UK Naval Bases and at Gibraltar, are easily identified by their black hulls, buff coloured superstructure and by the RMAS flag, which is a blue ensign defaced in the fly by a yellow anchor over two wavy lines. Pennant numbers are painted only on those vessels that are normally employed outside harbour limits.

The Marine Services became a Defence Agency on 1st April 1994 and throughout 1995, in addition to delivering its normal services, the Marine Services organisation has been involved in a much discussed "Market Testing" exercise, as part of the Government's "Competing for Quality" initiative. This has involved bidding for three areas of the business -in competition with industry. These were the marine services at Portsmouth, Devonport and the Clyde; Moorings and Navigation Buoyage and Naval Armament freighting. The result of the competition will now be known in February 1996 -with the new organisation, be it "in house" or contractor operated, commencing in June '96.

During 1995 the whole of the Marine Services operation at both Portland and Rosyth ended - with a subsequent reduction in both vessels and manpower. Whatever organisation runs the service in "96 it will be "lean and mean" compared to a few years ago. The scene below of six RMAS vessels being used to move one RFA are unlikely to be seen again.

D HANNAFORD

SHIPS OF
THE ROYAL MARITIME AUXILIARY SERVICE
Pennant Numbers

Ship	Pennant Number	Ship	Pennant Number
CAMERON	A72	SALUKI	A182
MELTON	A83	ISABEL	A183
MENAI	A84	SALMOOR	A185
MEON	A87	SALMASTER	A186
MILFORD	A91	SALMAID	A187
FELICITY	A112	SETTER	A189
MAGNET	A114	JOAN	A190
LODESTONE	A115	JOYCE	A193
CAIRN	A126	GWENDOLINE	A196
TORRENT	A127	SEALYHAM	A197
DALMATIAN	A129	HELEN	A198
TORNADO	A140	MYRTLE	A199
TORCH	A141	SPANIEL	A201
TORMENTOR	A142	NANCY	A202
TOREADOR	A143	NORAH	A205
WATERMAN	A146	LLANDOVERY	A207
FRANCES	A147	LAMLASH	A208
FIONA	A148	LECHLADE	A211
FLORENCE	A149	BEE	A216
GENEVIEVE	A150	FORCEFUL	A221
GEORGINA	A152	NIMBLE	A222
DEERHOUND	A155	POWERFUL	A223
DAPHNE	A156	ADEPT	A224
LOYAL HELPER	A157	BUSTLER	A225
SUPPORTER	A158	CAPABLE	A226
ELKHOUND	A162	CAREFUL	A227
GOOSANDER	A164	FAITHFUL	A228
POCHARD	A165	COCKCHAFER	A230
KATHLEEN	A166	DEXTEROUS	A231
KITTY	A170	ADAMANT	A232
LESLEY	A172	SHEEPDOG	A250
LILAH	A174	LYDFORD	A251
MARY	A175	LADYBIRD	A253
EDITH	A177	MEAVEY	A254
HUSKY	A178	(SULTAN VENTURER)	
MASTIFF	A180	CICALA	A263
IRENE	A181	SCARAB	A272

Ship	Pennant Number	Ship	Pennant Number
ILCHESTER	A308	FINTRY	A394
INSTOW	A309	GRASMERE	A402
BASSET	A327	CROMARTY	A488
COLLIE	A328	DORNOCH	A490
IMPULSE	A344	ROLLICKER	A502
IMPETUS	A345	HEADCORN	A1766
FELSTED	A348	HEVER	A1767
ELKSTONE	A353	HARLECH	A1768
EPWORTH	A355	HAMBLEDON	A1769
ROYSTERER	A361	HOLMWOOD	A1772
DENMEAD	A363	HORNING	A1773
FULBECK	A365	WATERSPOUT	Y19
ROBUST	A366	OILPRESS	Y21
NEWTON	A367	OILWELL	Y23
WARDEN	A368	OILBIRD	Y25
KINTERBURY	A378	OILMAN	Y26
CRICKLADE	A381	WATERCOURSE	Y30
ARROCHAR	A382	WATERFOWL	Y31
APPLEBY	A383	MOORHEN	Y32
CLOVELLY	A389	MOORFOWL	Y33
DUNSTER	A393		

RMAS Robust

ROYSTERER CLASS

Ship	Pennant Number	Completion Date	Builder
ROYSTERER	A361	1972	C.D. Holmes
ROBUST	A366	1974	C.D. Holmes
ROLLICKER	A502	1973	C.D. Holmes

G.R.T. 1,036 tons **Dimensions** 54m x 12m x 6m **Speed** 15 knots **Complement** 21.

Notes

Built for salvage and long range towage, a role they only fulfil infrequently. They are, however, used for various "deepwater" trials for MOD research departments. ROYSTERER was laid up in Portsmouth in 1995 and was expected to be sold by early 1996.

● H BALLARD

RMAS Impulse

IMPULSE CLASS

Ship	Pennant Number	Completion Date	Builder
IMPULSE	A344	1993	Dunston
IMPETUS	A345	1993	Dunston

G.R.T. 400 tons approx **Dimensions** 33m x 10m x 4m **Speed** 12 knots **Complement** 5.

Notes
Two new tugs completed in 1993 to serve as berthing tugs for the Trident Class submarines at Faslane.

RMAS Powerful

HARBOUR TUGS
TWIN UNIT TRACTOR TUGS (TUTT'S)

Ship	Pennant Number	Completion Date	Builder
FORCEFUL	A221	1985	R. Dunston
NIMBLE	A222	1985	R. Dunston
POWERFUL	A223	1985	R. Dunston
ADEPT	A224	1980	R. Dunston
BUSTLER	A225	1981	R. Dunston
CAPABLE	A226	1981	R. Dunston
CAREFUL	A227	1982	R. Dunston
FAITHFUL	A228	1985	R. Dunston
DEXTEROUS	A231	1986	R. Dunston

G.R.T. 375 tons **Dimensions** 39m x 10m x 4m **Speed** 12 knots **Complement** 9.

Notes
The principal harbour tug in naval service. CAPABLE is at Gibraltar.

RMAS Sheepdog

DOG CLASS

Ship	Pennant Number	Ship	Pennant Number
CAIRN ●	A126	SETTER	A189
DALMATIAN	A129	SEALYHAM	A197
DEERHOUND	A155	SPANIEL	A201
ELKHOUND	A162	SHEEPDOG	A250
HUSKY	A178	BASSET	A327
MASTIFF	A180	COLLIE ●	A328
SALUKI	A182		

G.R.T. 152 tons **Dimensions** 29m x 8m x 4m **Speed** 12 knots **Complement** 5.

Notes

General harbour tugs – all completed between 1962 and 1972.

● No longer tugs. Refitted as trials vessels for service at Kyle of Lochalsh.

Replacements for this class are due - a smaller version of the IMPULSE class is proposed (with a 30 tonnes bollard pull) when/if funding is secured. LABRADOR, FOXHOUND and CORGI sold 1995.

RMAS Daphne

IMPROVED GIRL CLASS

Ship	Pennant Number
DAPHNE	A156

G.R.T. 75 tons **Speed** 10 knots **Complement** 4.

Notes
Completed 1971-2. DAISY, DORIS, CHARLOTTE and CHRISTINE sold 1989, DOROTHY in 1990 and EDITH in 1995. DAPHNE laid up in reserve.

RMAS Joan

IRENE CLASS

Ship	Pennant Number	Ship	Pennant Number
KATHLEEN	A166	ISABEL	A183
KITTY	A170	JOAN	A190
LESLEY	A172	JOYCE ●	A193
LILAH	A174	MYRTLE	A199
MARY	A175	NANCY ●	A202
IRENE ●	A181	NORAH	A205

G.R.T. 89 tons **Speed** 8 knots **Complement** 4.

Notes
Known as Water Tractors these craft are used for basin moves and towage of light barges. ● For disposal 1996

RMAS Fiona

FELICITY CLASS

Ship	Pennant Number
FELICITY	A112
FRANCES	A147
FIONA	A148
FLORENCE	A149

Ship	Pennant Number
GENEVIEVE	A150
GEORGINA	A152
GWENDOLINE	A196
HELEN	A198

G.R.T. 80 tons **Speed** 10 knots **Complement** 4.

Notes
Water Tractors – completed in 1973; FRANCES, FLORENCE and GENEVIEVE completed 1980.

RMAS Newton

RESEARCH VESSEL

Ship	Pennant Number	Completion Date	Builder
NEWTON	A367	1976	Scotts

G.R.T. 2,779 tons **Dimensions** 99m x 16m x 6m **Speed** 15 knots **Complement** 39

Notes

An underwater research vessel with a limited cable laying capability.
Employed by the Defence Research Agency. AURICULA was sold for commercial service in 1995.

RMAS Arrochar

ARMAMENT STORES CARRIERS

Ship	Pennant Number	Completion Date	Builder
KINTERBURY	A378	1980	Appledore SB
ARROCHAR	A382	1981	Appledore SB

G.R.T. 1,357 tons **Dimensions** 64m x 12m x 5m **Speed** 14 knots **Complement** 19.

Notes

2 holds carry Naval armament stores, ammunition and guided missiles. Both vessels vary slightly. ARROCHAR (ex ST GEORGE) taken over in late 1988 from the Army. Both vessels have enough employment within the RMAS for the foreseeable future.

RMAS Bee

INSECT CLASS

Ship	Pennant Number	Completion Date	Builder
BEE	A216	1970	C.D. Holmes
COCKCHAFER	A230	1971	Beverley
LADYBIRD	A253	1973	Beverley
CICALA	A263	1971	Beverley
SCARAB	A272	1973	Beverley

G.R.T. 279 tons **Dimensions** 34m x 8m x 3m **Speed** 10.5 knots **Complement** 7-9.

Notes
SCARAB is fitted as a Mooring Vessel and COCKCHAFER as a Trials Stores Carrier – remainder are Naval Armament carriers.

LOYAL CLASS

Ship	Pennant Number	Ship	Pennant Number
LOYAL HELPER	A157	SUPPORTER	A158

G.R.T. 112 tons **Dimensions** 24m x 6m x 3m **Speed** 10.5 knots **Complement** 24.

Notes

These craft were operated by the Royal Naval Auxiliary Service (RNXS). It was decided however in 1993 that their role was no longer needed and the service was disbanded on 31st March 1994. LOYAL CHANCELLOR & LOYAL WATCHER were transferred to RN University units (see Page 37). LOYAL VOLUNTEER, L. PROCTOR and L. MODERATOR sold for commercial service in 1994. These vessels may be sold in 1996.

● FBM (COWES)

RMAS Adamant

ADAMANT

Ship	Pennant Number	Completion Date	Builder
ADAMANT	A232	1992	FBM (Cowes)

GRT 170 tonnes **Dimensions** 30m x 8m x 1m **Speed** 22 knots **Complement** 5

Notes

Twin catamaran hulls based on the commercial Red Jet design (as used by Red Funnel Ferry Co). First water jet propulsion vessel in the RMAS. In service as a Clyde personnel ferry.

RMAS Dornoch

(TYPE A, B & X) TENDERS

Ship	Pennant Number	Ship	Pennant Number
MELTON	A83	FULBECK	A365
MENAI	A84	CRICKLADE §	A381
MEON	A87	DUNSTER	A393
MILFORD	A91	FINTRY §	A394
LLANDOVERY	A207	GRASMERE	A402
LAMLASH	A208	DORNOCH	A490
LECHLADE	A211	HEADCORN	A1766
LYDFORD §	A251	HEAVER	A1767
ILCHESTER •	A308	HARLECH	A1768
INSTOW •	A309	HAMBLEDON	A1769
FELSTED	A348	HOLMWOOD	A1772
ELKSTONE	A353	HORNING	A1773
EPWORTH	A355		

G.R.T. 78 tons **Dimensions** 24m x 6m x 3m **Speed** 10.5 knots **Complement** 4/5.

Notes

All completed since 1971 to replace Motor Fishing Vessels. Vessels marked • are diving tenders. Remainder are Training Tenders, Passenger Ferries, or Cargo Vessels. CLOVELLY and CROMARTY sold 1994, CRICCIETH and GLENCOE in 1995. DENMEAD with RNR at Belfast. MEAVEY (A254) operates for HMS SULTAN as SULTAN VENTURER. § - For disposal 1996.

RMAS Oilwell

COASTAL OILERS
OILPRESS CLASS

Ship	Pennant Number	Completion Date	Builder
OILPRESS	Y21	1969	Appledore Shipbuilders
OILWELL	Y23	1969	Appledore Shipbuilders
OILBIRD	Y25	1969	Appledore Shipbuilders
OILMAN	Y26	1969	Appledore Shipbuilders

G.R.T. 362 tons **Dimensions** 41m x 9m x 3m **Speed** 11 knots **Complement** 5.

Notes
Employed as Harbour and Coastal Oilers. OILSTONE sold 17 Dec 92.

RMAS Waterman

WATER CARRIERS
WATER CLASS

Ship	Pennant Number	Completion Date	Builder
WATERSPOUT §	Y19	1967	Drypool Eng Co
WATERCOURSE	Y30	1974	Drypool Eng Co
WATERFOWL	Y31	1974	Drypool Eng Co
WATERMAN	A146	1978	R. Dunston

G.R.T. 263 tons **Dimensions** 40m x 8m x 2m **Speed** 11 knots **Complement** 5.

Notes
Capable of coastal passages, these craft normally supply either demineralised or fresh water to the Fleet within port limits. § - for disposal 1996.

RMAS Lodestone

DEGAUSSING VESSELS
MAGNET CLASS

Ship	Pennant Number	Completion Date	Builder
MAGNET	A114	1979	Cleland
LODESTONE	A115	1980	Cleland

G.R.T. 828 tons **Dimensions** 55m x 12m x 4m **Speed** 14 knots **Complement** 9.

Notes

LODESTONE is operational (on the Clyde). MAGNET in reserve (Portsmouth). A decision is still awaited re possible conversion of one vessel into a Diving Training Ship.

RMAS Torrent

TORPEDO RECOVERY VESSELS (TRV'S)
TORRID CLASS

Ship	Pennant Number	Completion Date	Builder
TORRENT	A127	1971	Cleland SB Co

G.R.T. 550 tons **Dimensions** 46m x 9m x 3m **Speed** 12 knots **Complement** 14.

Notes
A stern ramp is built for the recovery of torpedoes fired for trials and exercises. A total of 32 can be carried.

RMAS Tormentor

TORNADO CLASS

Ship	Pennant Number	Completion Date	Builder
TORNADO	A140	1979	Hall Russell
TORCH §	A141	1980	Hall Russell
TORMENTOR	A142	1980	Hall Russell
TOREADOR §	A143	1980	Hall Russell

G.R.T. 560 tons **Dimensions** 47m x 8m x 3m **Speed** 14 knots **Complement** 13.

Notes
TORMENTOR is based at Plymouth – remainder on the Clyde. All vessels have had suitable rails fitted to enable them to operate as exercise minelayers. § - In reserve - one for dispoal in 1996.

79

RMAS Salmaid

MOORING & SALVAGE VESSELS
SAL CLASS

Ship	Pennant Number	Completion Date	Builder
SALMOOR	A185	1985	Hall Russell
SALMASTER	A186	1986	Hall Russell
SALMAID	A187	1986	Hall Russell

Displacement 2200 tonnes **Dimensions** 77m x 15m x 4m **Speed** 15 knots **Complement** 17.

Notes
Multi-purpose vessels designed to lay and maintain underwater targets and moorings and undertake a wide range of salvage tasks.

RMAS Goosander

WILD DUCK CLASS

Ship	Pennant Number	Completion Date	Builder
GOOSANDER	A164	1973	Robb Caledon

G.R.T. 900 tons* **Dimensions** 58mm x 12m x 4m **Speed** 10 knots **Complement** 18.

Notes
Capable of carrying out a wide range of duties laying moorings and heavy lift salvage work. 200 tons can be lifted over the bow. In reserve (at Portsmouth). POCHARD was sold in 1995.

RMAS Moorfowl

MOOR CLASS

Ship	Pennant Number	Completion Date	Builder
MOORHEN	Y32	1989	McTay Marine
MOORFOWL	Y33	1989	McTay Marine
CAMERON	A72	1991	Richard Dunston

Displacement 518 tons **Dimensions** 32m x 11m x 2m **Speed** 8 knots **Complement** 10

Notes
Powered mooring lighters for use within sheltered coastal waters. (MOORHEN at Portsmouth, MOORFOWL at Devonport). CAMERON is similar but is employed as an Underwater Trials & Experimental vessel at Rosyth.

RMAS Warden

WARDEN CLASS

Ship	Pennant Number	Completion Date	Builder
WARDEN	A368	1989	Richards

Displacement 626 tons **Dimensions** 48m x 10m x 4m **Speed** 15 knots **Complement** 11.

Notes
Range Maintenance Vessel working on the RAE Aberporth range (S. Wales). Based at Pembroke Dock. Fitted with 30 tonne bollard pull towing winch to provide alternative employment for her.

The Directorate of Marine Services (Naval) is responsible for the provision of marine support for both RAF training and range safety/clearance duties at Army and MoD ranges throughout Britain. Such services are currently delivered under two separate Government Owned/Commercially Operated (GO/CO) contracts. Management of the contracts and overall provision of the service remains the responsibility of DMS(N).

The primary tasks for RAF Support craft include target towing, winch training helicopter crews for SAR and the vessels are also used for sea survivial training of aircrew. Details of RAF Support Craft are as follows:

LONG RANGE RECOVERY AND SUPPORT CRAFT (LRRSC)

Ship	Pennant Number	Completion Date	Builder
SEAL	5000	1967	Brooke Marine
SEAGULL	5001	1970	Fairmile Const.

G.R.T. 251 tons **Dimensions** 36.6m x 7.16mx 1.8m **Speed** 21 knots **Complement** 8. Both are based at Invergordon.

RESCUE AND TARGET TOWING LAUNCHES (RTTL)

SPITFIRE, HALIFAX, HAMPDEN, HURRICANE, LANCASTER & WELLINGTON

G.R.T. 60 tons **Dimensions** 24m x 5.6m x 1.6m **Speed** 21 knots **Complement** 4/6 They are based at Great Yarmouth and Plymouth.

There are also 3 x 63' Pinnaces Nos 1374, 1389 & 1392.
These craft are employed on target towing, SAR training, sea survival drills and various trials and weapon recovery. They are based at Holyhead and Plymouth.

Details of Range Safety Craft are as follows:

Ship	Pennant Number	Completion Date	Builder
FALCONET	Y01	1983	James & Stone
PETARD	Y02	1983	James & Stone

G.R.T. 60 tons **Dimensions** 24m x 5.5m x 1.5m **Speed** 21 knots **Complement** 6. They are based at Benbecula and Pembroke Dock.

Falconet

There are also eleven smaller range safety craft; details below:

Ship	Pennant Number	Ship	Pennant Number
JAMES DALTON VC	7822	GEOFFREY RACKHAM GC	8487
SAMUEL MORLEY VC	7713	RICHARD MASTERS VC	7820
JOSEPH HUGHES GC	7821	SIR CECIL SMITH	8126
SIR PAUL TRAVERS	8125	WALTER CLEALL GC	8488
SIR REGINALD KERR	8128	SIR EVAN GIBB	8489
SIR HUMPHREY GALE	8129		

G.R.T. 32.7 tonnes **Dimensions** 14.9m x 4.66m x 1.67m. **Speed** 22 knots **Complement** 3.

Their primary tasks are range surveillance and clearance in coastal range areas and sea danger areas. The craft are based at Pembroke Dock, Portland, Dover, Whitehaven and Loch Boisdale.

● C. HOCKADAY

ARMY LANDING CRAFT
LCL CLASS (LANDING CRAFT LOGISTIC)

Vessel	Pennant Number	Completion Date	Builder
HMAV ARDENNES	L4001	1977	Brooke Marine
HMAV ARAKAN	L4003	1978	Brooke Marine

Displacement 1,050 tons **Dimensions** 72m x 15m x 2m **Speed** 10 knots **Complement** 36.

Notes
Designed to carry up to 520 tonnes of cargo, overside loaded, or up to Five Chieftain tanks – Ro Ro loaded, reducing to 254 tonnes for beaching operations, through bow doors. Principal roles are maintenance of the Royal Artillery Range Outer Hebrides and in support of Amphibious Operations and Exercises.

RCTV Audemer

RCL CLASS
(RAMPED CRAFT LOGISTIC)

Vessel	Pennant Number	Completion Date	Builder
RCTV ANDALSNES	L107	1984	James & Stone
RCTV AKYAB	L109	1984	James & Stone
RCTV AACHEN	L110	1986	James & Stone
RCTV AREZZO	L111	1986	James & Stone
RCTV ARROMANCHES	L112	1987	James & Stone
RCTV AUDEMER	L113	1987	James & Stone

Displacement 165 tons **Dimensions** 33m x 8m x 1.5m **Speed** 9 knots **Complement** 6.

Notes
Smaller – "all purpose" landing craft capable of carrying up to 100 tons. In service in coastal waters around Cyprus and UK. ARROMANCHES was formerly AGHEILA (re-named 1994 when original vessel was sold).

Appleby

SEA CADET VESSELS

FLEET TENDERS 63 DESIGN

Ship	Pennant Number	Ship	Pennant Number
ALNMOUTH	Y13	APPLEBY	A383

Displacement 117 tons **Dimensions** 24m x 5m x 3m **Speed** 10.5 knots.

Notes
'Craft are allocated to the Sea Cadet Corps and are used by units throughout the UK.
ALNMOUTH and APPLEBY brought up to DTI standards and returned to service mid '94. ABERDOREY and ABINGER sold in 1995.
Ex-BIBURY (A103) operates for Portsmouth Naval Base Sub Aqua Club.

British Aerospace Sea Harrier

Variants: F/A 2

Role: Short take off, vertical landing (STOVL) fighter attack and reconnaissance aircraft.

Engine: 1 x 21,500lb thrust Rolls Royce PEGASUS 104, turbofan.

Span 25' 3" **Length** 49' 1" **Height** 12' 0" **Max weight** 26,200lb.

Max speed Mach .9 540 knots **Crew** 1 pilot.

Avionics: Blue Vixen pulse doppler radar

Armament: Up to 4 x AMRAAM Air to Air Missiles. SEA EAGLE air to surface missiles. SIDEWINDER air to air missiles. 2 - 30mm Aden cannons with 120 rounds per gun in detachable pods, one either side of the lower fuselage. 1 fuselage centreline and 4 underwing hardpoints. The inner wing stations are capable of carrying 2,000lb of stores and are plumbed for drop tanks. The other positions can carry stores up to 1,000lb in weight. Possible loads include 1,000lb or practice bombs; BL 755 cluster bombs, 190 or 100 gallon drop tanks. A single F95 camera can be mounted obliquely in the nose for reconnaissance.

Squadron Service: 800, 801 and 899 squadrons in commission.

Notes: During 1996, 800 squadron will be embarked in HMS INVINCIBLE and 801 in HMS ILLUSTRIOUS. 899 squadron is responsible for the training of pilots and maintainers and the development of tactics.It is normally shore based at Yeovilton. In a period of tension it could embark to reinforce the embarked air groups in the carriers.

OFFICIAL PHOTO

Westland SEA KING

Developed for the Royal Navy from the Sikorsky SH3D, the basic Sea King airframe is used in three different roles. The following details are common to all:
Engines: 2 x 1600shp Rolls Royce Gnome H 1400 – 1 free power turbines.
Rotor Diameter 62' 0" **Length** 54' 9" **Height** 17' 2" **Max Weight** 21,400lb **Max Speed** 125 knots.
The 3 versions are:-

OFFICIAL PHOTO

SAR MK 5 : HAS 6

The HAS6 has improved sonics, deeper dipping active sonar and ESM
Roles: Anti-submarine search and strike. SAR. Transport.
Crew: 2 pilots, 1 observer and 1 aircrewman.
Avionics: Sea Searcher radar; Type 2069 variable depth active/passive sonar AQS 902 passive sonobuoy analyser. Orange Crop passive ESM equipment.
Armament: 4 fuselage hardpoints capable of carrying STINGRAY torpedoes or depth charges. Various flares, markers, grenades and sonobuoys can be carried internally and hand launched. A 7.62mm machine gun can be mounted in the doorway.
Squadron Service: 771 Squadron operates an SAR 5.706, 810, 814, 819, and 820 squadrons are in commission equipped with HAS 6.
Notes: The Sea King has been the backbone of the Fleet Air Arm's anti-submarine force since 1970. 706 is the advanced training squadron at Culdrose. 810 is an operational flying training squadron with the capability to embark to reinforce the front line. During 1996, 814 squadron will be embarked in HMS INVINCIBLE and 820 in HMS ILLUSTRIOUS. 819 is shore based at Prestwick The SAR 5 has an excellent SAR capability which is frequently demonstrated in the south west approaches. The HAS 6 has less complete SAR facilities when full ASW equipment fitted.

AEW 2

Role: Airborne Early Warning. **Crew:** 1 pilot and 2 observers.
Avionics: Thorn/EMI Searchwater radar Orange Crop passive ESM equipment.
Squadron Service: 849 HQ, 849A and 849B flights in commission.
Notes: Used to detect low flying aircraft trying to attack aircraft carrier battle groups under conventional shipborne radar cover. Can also be used for surface search utilising its sophisticated, computerised long range radar. During 1996 849A flight will be embarked in HMS INVINCIBLE and 849B in HMS ILLUSTRIOUS 849HQ acts as a training and trials unit at Culdrose.

HC 4

Role: Commando assault and utility transport.
Crew: 2 pilots and 1 aircrewman.
Armament: Door mounted 7.62mm machine gun.
Squadron Service: 845 , 846 and 848 squadrons in commission.
Notes: The HC4 has a fixed undercarriage with no sponsons or radome.Can carrying up to 27 troops in the cabin or underslung loads up to 8,000lb in weight. All squadrons are based at Yeovilton but embark or detatch at short notice to support 3 Cdo Brigade.845 Sqdn has spent long periods in Split in support of UN Forces in Bosnia since1993.

Westland LYNX

Variants: HAS 3, HAS 3S, HMA 8.
Roles: Surface search and strike; anti-submarine strike; SAR.
Engines: 2 x 900hp Rolls Royce GEM BS 360-07-26 free shaft turbines.
Rotor diameter: 42' 0" **Length** 39' 1" **Height** 11' 0" **Max Weight** 9,500lb.
Max Speed: 150 knots. **Crew:** 1 pilot and 1 observer.
Avionics: SEA SPRAY radar. Orange Crop passive ESM equipment. Sea Owl PID (Mk 8)
Armament: External pylons carry up to 4 - SEA SKUA air to surface missiles or 2 x STINGRAY, Mk 46 torpedoes, depth charges, flares or markers.
Squadron Service: 702 and 815 squadrons in commission.

Notes: 815 OEU FLT is a trials squadron with equipment for HMA 8 and 702 is a training squadron based at Portland. 815 squadron also based at Portland is the parent unit for single aircraft ships flights. A "military" version of the Lynx, the AH7 is operated by 847 NAS which is based at Yeovilton.
The HMA Mk 8 is now flying and undergoing intensive development trials. Full delivery of 44 conversions expected by 2003.

Westland GAZELLE HT2

Engine: 1 x 592shp Turbomeca ASTAZOU free power turbine.
Crew: 1 or 2 pilots.

Notes: In service with 705 squadron at Culdrose. Used for training all RN helicopter pilots up to "wings standard" before they move onto the Sea King or Lynx. A version of the Gazelle, the AH1, is used by 847 NAS based at Yeovilton as a spotter/communications aircraft.

OTHER AIRCRAFT TYPES IN ROYAL NAVY SERVICE DURING 1996

British Aerospace JETSTREAM T2 and T3

Engines: 2 x 940hp Turbomeca ASTAZOU 16D turboprops. (T3 Garrett turboprops).
Crew: 1 or 2 pilots, 2 student observers plus 3 other seats.
Notes: T2's are used by 750 squadron at Culdrose for training Fleet Air Arm Observers.T3's are used by the Heron flight at Yeovilton for operational support/communications flying.

GROB G115 D-2

Has taken over the flying grading and conversion of Rotory to Fixed Wing flying task from the Chipmunk. They are owned and operated by a division of Short Brothers plc. They operate from Plymouth City Airport.

British Aerospace HAWK

Engine: 1 x Ardour Mk 151 5200 lbs thrust.
Crew: 1 or 2 Pilots (both service and civilian)
Notes: With FRADU at Culdrose to provide support for training of RN ships, RN flying standards flight and as airborne targets for the aircraft direction school.

Royal Navy Historic Flight

The RNHF is undergoing a period of change and had to become financed independently from the RN during 1995. A trust has been set up to provide funds from individuals and industry. The current holding of aircraft is:
Flying: 2 Fairey Swordfish, 1 Fairey Firefly
Static Display: 1 Fairey Swordfish
Under refurbishment at BAe Brough: 1 Hawker Sea Fury
Also held is a Hawker Sea Hawk which it is hoped to refurbish to flying condition at BAe Dunsfold..

Full details of these and many other naval aircraft can be found in the revised edition of AIRCRAFT OF THE ROYAL NAVY SINCE 1945 published by Maritime Books.

At the end of the line ...

Readers may well find other warships afloat which are not mentioned in this book. The majority have fulfilled a long and useful life and are now relegated to non-seagoing duties. The following list gives details of their current duties:

Pennant Number	Ship	Remarks
A134	RAME HEAD	Escort Maintenance Vessel – Royal Marines Training Ship at Portland
C35	BELFAST	World War II Cruiser Museum ship – Pool of London Open to the public daily Tel: 0171-407 6434
D23	BRISTOL	Type 82 Destroyer – Sea Cadet Training Ship at Portsmouth.
D73	CAVALIER	World War II Destroyer Museum Ship at Hebburn Not open to public. Future under consideration.
F126	PLYMOUTH	Type 12 Frigate & Oberon class Submarine Museum Ships at Birkenhead
S21	ONYX	Open to the public daily. Tel: 0151 650 1573
M1115	BRONINGTON	Ton Class Minesweeper Manchester Limited Opening to the Public Tel 0161 877 7778
S67	ALLIANCE	Submarine – Museum Ship at Gosport Open to the public daily. Tel: 01705 511485
M1151	IVESTON	(Thurrock) } Static Sea
M1154	KELLINGTON	(Stockton upon Tees) } Cadet Training
M1200	SOBERTON	(Erith) } Vessels

At the time of publishing the following ships were awaiting tow for scrap or sale.

PORTSMOUTH		ROSYTH	PLYMOUTH
Jupiter	Sirius	Churchill	Conqueror
Scylla	Hermione	Dreadnought	Courageous
Brinton	Sheraton	Revenge	Warspite
Wilton	Redpole	Swiftsure	Valiant
Cygnet	Kingfisher	Resolution	
	Kent		

96